For Jimmy George

BLOOMSBURY CHILDREN'S BOOKS
Bloomsbury Publishing Plc
50 Bedford Square, London, WC1B 3DP, UK

BLOOMSBURY, BLOOMSBURY CHILDREN'S BOOKS and the Diana logo are
trademarks of Bloomsbury Publishing Plc

First published in Great Britain 2019 by Bloomsbury Publishing Plc

A catalogue record for this book is available from the British Library

ISBN: HB: 978-1-4088-9922-9, PB: 978-1-4088-9921-2, eBook: 978-1-5266-0561-0

2 4 6 8 10 9 7 5 3 1 (hardback), 2 4 6 8 10 9 7 5 3 1 (paperback)

Printed and bound in China by Leo Paper Products, Heshan, Guangdong

All papers used by Bloomsbury Plc are natural, recyclable products from wood grown in well managed forests.
The manufacturing process conform to the environmental regulations of the country of origin

To find out more about our authors and books visit www.bloomsbury.com and sign up for our newsletters
To find out more about Katie Abey visit www.katieabey.co.uk

WE EAT BANANAS

KATIE ABEY

BLOOMSBURY
CHILDREN'S BOOKS
LONDON OXFORD NEW YORK NEW DELHI SYDNEY

We Eat Apples, Oranges and Pears

Find your **favourite** fruit at the market.